Hercules Henry Graves MacDonnell

A Book of Dates, Operatic, Dramatic and Musical

Hercules Henry Graves MacDonnell

A Book of Dates, Operatic, Dramatic and Musical

ISBN/EAN: 9783337342036

Printed in Europe, USA, Canada, Australia, Japan

Cover: Foto ©Thomas Meinert / pixelio.de

More available books at **www.hansebooks.com**

A BOOK OF DATES,

OPERATIC, DRAMATIC,

AND

MUSICAL.

COMPILED FOR

THE STROLLERS:

—————•>o<•————

DUBLIN:

BROWNE AND NOLAN, NASSAU-STREET.

1878.

My Dear Strollers,

In this condensed List of Dates, it would be impossible to notice everything which deserves to be noticed. I have had to omit and to select, in order to be brief.

The selection has been made with a view to settling the discussions and answering the inquiries so frequently made at the pleasant Meetings of the Musical Members of the Strollers.

I have also necessarily been influenced by the extent of my own Memoranda, which I have been able to find, of the various Musical events, from the time of my entrance into College, in 1835, "Quorum pars magna fui."

Yours, &c.,

HERCULES MacDONNELL.

January, 1878.

DATES,

OPERATIC, DRAMATIC, AND MUSICAL,

DUBLIN.*

A.D.

1634   The first Theatre opened in Dublin by JOHN OGILBY in *Werburgh Street*.
This afterwards closed by order of the Lords Justices.

1662   OGILBY opened *Smock Alley Theatre* on what is now Essex Street.

1731   A Music Hall opened in *Crow Street*.

1732   Madame VIOLANTE (having previously opened a Booth in *Fownes' Court*, where PEG WOFFINGTON first appeared) removed to *George's Lane*, now South Great George's Street.   Closed.

1734   March—ELRINGTON opened *Aungier Street Theatre*, corner of Longford Street,

1735   *Smock Alley Theatre* rebuilt.

1740† *Catch Club* founded about this time by the Vicars Choral of the two Cathedrals.

Anacreontic Society founded.

1741   A Music Hall built in *Fishamble Street*.
George Fred. Handel arrived November 18th, and produced here—
December 23rd—*Acis and Galatea, L'Allegro, &c., Ode to St. Cecilia*.

---

* It should be observed that *first* appearances and *first* productions of any importance are generally printed in Italics.

† This date rests on a vague tradition, the records of the Club not going further back than 1770; but by some a Society, or Glee Club, is thought to have been in existence so far back as 1700, from which arose the present "Catch Club."

A.D.

1742 April 13th—*Messiah*.* February—*Esther*. May 25th—*Saul*, Dr. ARNE subsequently gave Concerts in this Music Hall.

1753 *Beef Steak Club* founded.

1758 October 23rd—*Crow Street Theatre* opened, under SPRANGER BARRY, on site of Crow Street Music Hall.

1781 *John Philip Kemble* at "Smock Alley."

1786 The Act 26 Geo. III., cap. 57, was passed for regulating the Stage in the city and county of Dublin. The Crown is enabled to grant patents for 21 years on such conditions as it may think proper. Any person performing in an unauthorized place is liable to £300 fine, except in the Rotunda, for the benefit of the Hospital; and also excepting horsemanship, puppet shows, and the like.

1787 *Irish Musical Fund Society* founded.

1788 Mrs. *Jordan* appeared as Miss FRANCIS.

1790 "Smock Alley" given up; became a Corn Store, and in 1815 site of Chapel of S.S. Michael and John.

1792 Fishamble Street Music Hall converted into a *Private* Theatre.

1803 *Sir John Stevenson* knighted.

1808 May 15th—*Michael William Balfe* born in Dublin at 10 Pitt Street.

1814 "Crow Street Riots"—"The Miller and his Men" being substituted for "The Forest of Bondy," with the trained dog, "Montargis."

1819 "Crow Street Riots" renewed and Theatre totally wrecked, on account of the Manager having cancelled Miss *Byrne's* engagement.

A fragment of it remains in the wall facing Fownes's Street; also a portion of the Scene Room in Temple Bar, afterwards a Hat factory, and then a stable.

* The Gentlemen of the two Choirs sang for HANDEL:—Soloists, Signor AVOLIO, Mr. CIBBER (appeared at Aungier Street Theatre, December 12th, 1841), Mr. CHURCH, Mr. ROSEINGRANE.

1820   Mr. *Henry Harris* purchased the site of the present *Theatre Royal*. The site was originally a meat market, and in 1796 the Royal Dublin Society built their house there. This is the present front to Hawkins Street. The room with a glass dome was probably a lecture room or drawing school. The wardrobe room, with the old original presses, was a library; the property room a mineral museum.

The Royal Dublin Society had removed, in 1815, to Leinster House, and in 1818 the Mendicity occupied Hawkins Street.

1821   January 18th—*Theatre Royal* completed and opened; HENRY HARRIS, Owner; Mr. *Beasley*, Architect. Cost about £50,000. H. HARRIS issued fifty *Debentures* of £200, and also mortgaged it to Mr. BICKNELL.

1st Night: " Comedy of Errors " and the " Sleepwalker,"— " Yorkshire" JOHNSTON; *Paul Bedford;* ALEXANDER LEE; P. FARREN, Stage Manager; MR. BARTON, Leader.

February 12th—*Charles Younge* as Hamlet.

March 16th—WILLIAM FARREN, School for Scandal.

July—*Miss. Catherine Stephens.*—Duruset.

August—*Charles Kemble.*

August 22nd—King George IV. at Theatre Royal—" Duenna" and " Patrick's Day" (Sheridan); Receipts, £600.

October 29th—*Girmaldi.*

1822   April—" *Tom and Jerry.*"

July 15th to August 12th—*Edmund Kean.*

November—*Liston.*

December—" The Bottle Riot " on visit of Lord Lieutenant— Lord Wellesley.

1823   January 4th—" Love in a Village,"—Miss STEPHENS, Mr. HORN, P. BEDFORD; A. LEE; A. LEE became Director and Leader.

June—*Braham.*

August—†*Catalani*—Three nights at Theatre Royal, but only in Concerts; sang " Non piu andrai " and " Nel cor piu non."

---

* Born 1794; daughter of Edward Stephens, of Leadwell, Oxford; 1838, married 5th Earl of Essex.

† ANGELICA CATALANI, born at Senigaglia, 1782; *debut* 1802; died at Paris, of cholera, June 13, 1849.

A.D.

1823　October—*Gas* first introduced at Theatre Royal.

1824　January—*Macready*—" Virginius."

October 23rd—*J. W. Calcraft* as " Joseph Surface;" afterwards lessee of Theatre Royal.

November—Madame *Vestris*, " Don Giovanni in London," and *Charles Mathews, Senior*.

1825　April 11th—*Vandenhoff* in Pizarro.

July—Miss *Foote* (Lady Harrington).

November—" Merry Wives of Windsor " (with music)—Miss STEPHENS, Miss FORDE, BRAHAM, and *Phillips*.

1826　July—TOM COOKE, Miss STEPHENS, WALLACK—" Faustus " produced.　Miss STEPHENS introduced " Faustus " (Mary); " I believed thee true " ! " The Brigand."

R. M. Levey directed to organize a band.

November—Mrs. *Waylett*.

December 30th—Miss *Paton* as " Polly " in the Beggar's Opera.

This year died Dr. SPRAY, the tenor, and INCLEDON.

Philharmonic Society founded.

1827　January 7—Miss PATON and PHILLIPS—Freyschutz—Love in a Village—Guy Mannering—Nozze—Haunted Tower—Maid of the Mill.

February 7th—*Oberon*—The Slave.

March—EDMUND KEAN.

August 2nd—" Messiah" at St. Patrick's—BUGGINE, MAGRATH, two *Robinsons (W. and F.)*, and SMITH (Mus. D.)

August 14th—Nine nights—*Pasta*, only in Songs, and last act of " Romeo," with CASTELLI.　BRAHAM :—

　　　　　" The Slave,"
　　　　　" Oberon,"
　　　　　" Artaxerxes,"
　　　　.　" Love in a Village."

Miss *Garbois* danced.

November 3rd—*Bunn* announced as lessee of the Theatre Royal.

A.D.

1827   November 27th—*Italian Opera*, that is Operas in English, with some Italian artistes, portions of the words being sung in Italian to suit their convenience, and Italian Songs and Duets introduced to suit their fancy—

" Barbiere,"	Madame *Carnega*,
" Pizarro,"	Miss KENNETH,
" Castle of Andalusia, &c.	Signor *Begrez*,
	Signor GIUBILEI,
	Mr. COOKE.

1828   January—" Italian Opera " Company continued.

April 2nd—Incorporated Irish Musical Fund had an " Annual Handel Commemoration " at Rotunda—" Messiah."

The Misses *Ash* were now the fashionable singers.

Mr. *Conran* played and accompanied.

The Beef Steak Club was disorganized by political dissensions and soon after given up.*

April 21st—*Charles Kean, Jun.* (1st), as Norval in "Douglas."

June 17th—Mr. LUKE PLUNKET encored in the death scene of Richard III ! then sang " Scots wha hae !"

September—Theatre Royal sank into a Circus—*Ducrow's.*

1829   January—Miss PATON, Mrs. WAYLETT, PHILLIPS.

April 29—Theatre opened in *Abbey Street by* Messrs. CALVERT.

May—Theatre Royal—two nights—CARADORI sang.

October 13th—First real *Italian Opera*, with English afterpiece. Boxes 5s.; Pit 3s.

" Il Fanatico,"	De Begnis, Curioni,
" Otello,"	ANGELI, GIUBILEI,
" Barbiere,"	Madame BLASIS, and CASTELLI.
" La Gazza,"	Leader, SPAGNOLETTI.

November 10th—English Opera :—

" The Devil's Bridge,"	Miss THORNE,
" *Masaniello*," Dec. 2nd,	Miss BYFIELD,
" Siege of Belgrade,"	Mr. BROUGH, PHILLIPS,
" Waterman,"	BRAHAM.

* The Lord Lieutenant (the Marquis of Wellesley), just before leaving Ireland, dined at the Club in Morrison's Hotel. Immediately after he left the room, Lord Rathdown, who was in the chair, proposed a toast, which has been somewhat variously reported, but of which the following seems a correct version :— " The Exports of Ireland ! A fair wind for them !! And may the enemies of the British Constitution be the first ! ! ! "

A.D.

1830 January—" The Hypocrite,"—*Dowton.*

May—Mr. *Wood* and Miss PATON.

Tyrone *Power.*

July 12th—CHARLES KEMBLE and daughter, *Fanny Kemble.*

August 21st—Mr. CALCRAFT became Lessee of Theatre Royal at £2,000 rent, also paying £250 to keep Queen's Theatre closed. He held for 16 years, and estimated his average expense at £15,000.

" Damon and Pythias," Mademoiselle *Celeste.*

1831 (Mrs. SIDDONS died in London.)

August 30th to September 3rd—*Dublin Musical Festival*—two Balls, two Concerts, two Oratorios at Theatre Royal ;—

" Triumph of Faith," by Ries.

Part of " Thanksgiving," Oratorio, by Stevenson.

" Messiah." Conductor, *Ferd. Ries.*

Violinist, *Paganini.* Cello, LINLEY. Vocalists, Mrs. KNYVETT, Madame STOCKHAUSEN, DE BEGNIS, BRAHAM, PHILLIPS. Tickets 15s.; Concert £1.

June—Madame VESTRIS.

" Teddy the Tyler," " Irish Tutor," &c.—POWER.

August—Mr. and Mrs. *Wood.*

" Adelphi," now *Queen's,* open " by consent of Mr. CALCRAFT."

1832 July—Report of Committee of House of Commons on the laws of " Dramatic Literature."

1833 The African Roscius, *Aldridge.*

April 9th—" A young gentleman of 14 " appeared and failed—*Gustavus V. Brooke.*

May 15th—(EDMUND KEAN died at Richmond.)

July—Ballet—*Taglioni* and SILVAIN.

September 14th—(Sir JOHN STEVENSON died at Headfort.)

1834 January—
" Love in a Village, "
" Paul Pry,"
{ Mrs. WAYLETT,
BEDFORD,
BROUGH,
JOHNSTON.

September 21st—Italian Opera—

" Barbiere,"
" Tancredi,"
" Otello,"
" Fanatico,"
" Semiramide,"
" D. Giovanni,"
{ Mesdames KINTHERLAND,
CESARI, and CRAMPINI ;
CURIONI, GIUBILEI,
A. Sapio, and DE BEGNIS.

A.D.

1834 October—*Dr. Joy* joined the company as Mr. RAY.

The "Antients" commenced their Meetings at Mr. (afterwards Dr.) FRANCIS ROBINSON's, 85 Lower Mount Street.*

December—" Eily O'Connor " (The Collegians) produced.

1835 R. M. LEVEY announced as " Director and Leader."

January—"Guy Mannering,"—BEDFORD, REES, Miss HYLAND, and HUDDART.

April—" Rivals,"
 " School for Scandal,"
  { WILLIAM FARREN, Miss HUDDART, Miss FAUCITT.

June—
 " The Mountain Sylph,"
  { Miss HYLAND, Miss A. HYLAND, WOOD, BROUGH.

October 10th—Mrs. WAYLETT.

November—CHARLES KEMBLE.

November 12th—French Company at Adelphi Theatre.

(CHARLES MATHEWS, Senr., died at Davenport.)

December 10th—The first " Antient Concert."

December—
 " Sonnambula,"
 " Freyschutz,"
  { Miss BIRCH, WILSON.

1836 January—POWER.

February 20th—Italian Opera (Twelve nights)—

 " Barbiere,"
 " Tancredi,"
 " *Donna del Lago*,"
 " *L'Italiana in Algieri*,"
 " Fanatico par la musica,"
 " Semiramide,"
 " Norma,"
 " Cenerentóla,"
 " Otello,"
 " *Sonnambula*,"
 " Don Giovanni,"
 " Puritani,"
  Madame D'ANGIOLI, Contessa DEGLI ANTONI, CURIONI, SAPIO, BERRETTONI, DE BEGNIS.

March—The Miss ASHES' " Annual Concert " at Rotunda.

April 4th—*Sheridan Knowles*—" Tell," " Hunchback."

June—Madame VESTRIS and CHARLES MATHEWS, Junr.

September 23rd—*Malibran*, having been engaged at Theatre Royal, died (age 28) at Morley Arms, Manchester.

* They then met at Mr. Schoales', Fitzwilliam Square, afterwards at Dawson Street, in the house now occupied by the Royal Irish Academy, until they removed in 1843 to the Antient Rooms in Brunswick Street.

A.D.

1836 October—Mr. and Mrs. Wood (Miss Paton), Henri Herz., P.F.

November—*University Choral Society* began Meetings at *Hercules MacDonnell's* Rooms, T.C.D.

Charles Graves (Bishop of Limerick), J. Graves, J. W. Laughlin, and H. Ringwood.

1837 January 2nd—Italian Opera—

"Cenerentola,"
"Prova d'une Opera seria," } Contessa Delgi Antoni,
"Gazza Ladra," } Signor De Val,
"Barbiere," } De Begnis.
"Sonnamula,"

January 6th—Concert—*Ole Bull*, Violin. Bochsa, Harp. Miss *Shirreff*, Templeton.

May 5th—"Jim Crow!" Mr. Rice.

———— Gustavus V. Brooke (succeeded).

———— Antient Society regularly and publicly founded.

November—*University Choral* founded (see 1836.)

1838 Power and Mrs. *Fitzwilliam*.

February 27th—Italian Opera Buffa, Madame Franceschini.

"Elisire," "Betly,"
"Nozze"—March 6th } Mesdemoiselles Scheroni, *Parigiani;*
"L'Italiana," } Catone, T., Bellini,
"Scaramuccia," } F. Lablache,
"Campanello," } Berrettoni.
"Elisae Claudio," } Mitchell.
"Sonnambula," April 7

(Stalls, 10s.; Boxes, 7s.; Pit 2s.)

April—Mr. Conran's Concert—Miss *Searles*.

June 16th—First Ladies' Concert, University Choral Society.

September 3rd—Two Concerts (Theatre Royal), and end of 1st and 3rd Acts of *Lucia*—*Persiani, Rubini, Nigri*.

November 6th—Madame Dulcken at Rotunda.

November 10th—English Opera—

"Sonnambula,"
"Barber,"
"Cinderella," } Balfe,
"Fra Diavolo," } Mr. and Mrs. Wood,
"Love in a Village," } Horncastle.
"Rob Roy,"
†"Amilie" (Nov. 21),

* Afterwards Madame Morosini.   † By the Irish Composer, Rooke.

1839 March—TYRONE POWER and Mrs. FITZWILLIAM. Last appearance of POWER in Dublin. (He was drowned in 1841, when returning from America in the "President ").

April—BOCHSA and *Mrs. Bishop* (afterwards Lady Bishop).

—— Abbey Street Theatre burned.

October—Theatre Royal. " *Maid of Artois*,"—Miss ROMER, TEMPLETON, A. SAPIO, BALFE.

Theatre Royal occupied by VAN AMBURGH and his Lions.

1840 Miss *Ellen Tree* (afterwards Mrs. C. Kean).

Mr. and Madame *Balfe*, Mrs. WAYLETT, HORNCASTLE.

Anacreontic Centenary Concert—*Liszt*.

October 19th—French Dramatic Company—Mons. CLOUSS, " Avant and Après "—" Passe minuit."

1841 January 7th—Rotunda Concerts with LISZT.

February—Miss ROMER, TEMPLETON, PHILLIPS.

February 21st—*Julia Cruise*, of Edinburgh (aunt of J. Cruise, Mrs. Levey), as Pauline, " Lady of Lyons."

April—" Amilie "—*Mr. and Mrs. Alban Croft*, Mr. FRAZER.

May 27th—Antient Concert, Rotunda.

—— (The " Tamburini Row," at Her Majesty's, London.)

May 29th—(PAGANINI died at Nice; born at Genoa, 1784 ; came to Paris and London, 1831.)

May 31st—Six nights at Theatre Royal—JULLIEN.

June 7th—Rotunda Concerts—LISZT.

August 30th (Eight nights)—Italian Opera—

" Puritani,"   ⎧ *Giulia Grisi, Mario,**
" Norma,"   ⎪ ERNESTA GRISI,
" Sonnambula,"   ⎨ *Labluche (sen.)*,
" La prova d'un Opera seria," ⎩ *Benedict*, Conductor.

August—JULLIEN at Portobello Gardens.

A Sacred Harmonic Society founded, Mr. MACLAGAN, Conductor.

October—Theatre Royal—ELLEN TREE and *Anderson*.

November 8th—Abbey Street "New Music Hall," opened by JAMES BARTON with Promenade Concerts.

November 13th—*Koenig* (Cornet) announced.

---

* GIOVANNI MARIO (Marchese di Candia) ; born at Cagliari, June 24th, 1809 ; *debut* Paris, December 1st, 1838, Robert ; London, 1840, Lucrezia. He used to say, " My career did not begin till I sang in Dublin."

A.D.

1842   April 23rd—" Acis and Galatea." LEVEY's Benefit.

May—English Opera—

" Nozze,"   *Adelaide Kemble,*
" Norma,"   Miss RAINSFORTH,
     Miss *Hyland,* BALFE,
     Weiss, BROUGH.

May—Helen FAUCITT.

September 5th to 18th—Italian Opera—

" Puritani,"
" Barbiere,'·   GRISI, ERNESTA GRISI,
" *Anna Bolena,*"   Madame F. LABLACHE,
" Elisire,"   LABLACHE (Sen.)
" Norma,"   *COSTA, Conductor.

(Boxes, 8s. ; Pit, 4s.)

November 28th—*Metropolitan Choral Society* founded—
Messrs. BUSSELL and LIDDELL, JOHN ROBINSON, WM. ELLIOTT
HUDSON, W. S. CONRAN, &c., were on the Committee.

December 5th—Anacreontic—*Thalberg,* PARRY.

(" Quanto amore ")—Madame and Signor *Ronconi.*

(THALBERG played one night at Theatre Royal.)

December 13th—Catch Club dined at Radley's Hotel.

1843   Madame VESTRIS, CHARLES MATHEWS, Mrs. GLOVER, Mrs.
FITZWILLIAM, *Buckstone.*

May—English Opera—

"Norma,"   Miss *Poole,*
" Lovespell,"   Mrs. ALFRED SHAW,
     SABELLA NOVELLO,
     Miss MANVERS, GIUBILEI.

(Dan) Leonard.

June 24th—Theatre Royal—HELEN FAUCITT.

August—Concert—*Sivori* and BALFE.

August 7th—(Six nights) English Opera—

" Norma,"   *Clara Novello,*
" Lovespell "   Miss Howson,
     Miss A. HYLAND,
     Madame ALBERTAZZI, BALFE.

August 28th—Ballet, " La Gizelle "—*Fanny Elssler,* Mons.
SILVAIN (Sullivan, really).

Madame CELESTE and WEBSTER.

---

* Afterwards Sir MICHAEL COSTA—knighted at Windsor, April 14th, 1869.

A.D.

1843 November 24th—The Antient Concert Society held their Meetings at the new "Antient Concert Rooms,"* Brunswick Street.

1844 English Opera—Miss RAINFORTH, *Eugene Garcia, W. Harrison,* STRETTON.

May 5th—Philharmonic met first time at Antient Rooms.

June—JOHN C. JOSEPHS purchased Patent of "Queen's."

Italian Opera, Theatre Royal—GRISI, *Favanti,* CORELLI, MARIO, F. LABLACHE.

CHARLES and *Mrs.* KEAN.

1845 January 29th—Philharmonic—THALBERG, PARRY, Miss BIRCH and DOLBY.

January 30th—At Theatre Royal.

February 4th—HELEN FAUCITT. February 22nd—*"Antigone,"* with Chorus.

March 24th—DAN LEONARD.

May 22nd and 24th—*Duprez* and EUGENE GARCIA at Theatre Royal Concert, and selections (in English) from "Lucia," and "William Tell."

July 7th—English Opera—

"Bohemian Girl," ⎫ Miss ROMER,
"Enchantress,"   ⎬ W. HARRISON,
"Daughter of St. Mark"⎭ *Borrani* (really M. Boisragou)

October 18th—English Opera—†*Simms Reeves,* Mr. and Mrs. ALBAN CROFT.

August 24th—Ballet—" Les Danseuses Viennoises."

November 3rd—Concerts—BRAHAM and his Son, H. and Miss BALFE.

December—Pantomime—" Blunderbore,"—J. F. WALLER.

1846 Ballet—*Carlotta Grisi.*

August 31st—Italian Opera (Eight nights)—

"Lucia," "Sonnambula,"⎫ *Castellan, Marras,*
" Belisario,"   ⎬ *Fornasari,*
" Puritani," " Norma,"⎭ *Ciabatta.*

* These had been the old Oil Gas Works. The Organ was built by Messrs. TELFORD in 1847, and the Dining room was added for the Catch Club in 1850.

† Born at Woolwich, 1818; made his debut on stage, as a baritone, at Newcastle, 1839.

A.D.

1846 October—Ballet—TAGLIONI.
<u>JOHN HARRIS</u> took " The Queen's."
Dublin Madrigal Society founded—G. GEARY, Conductor.

1847 January 20th—" Money,"—G. V. BROOKE.
" Iphigenia in Aulis,"—HELEN FAUCITT.
February—

" Maid of Artois,"
" Anna Bolena,"   } Madame *Anna Bishop*,
" Lovespell," " Sonnambula," } P. CORRI, Mr. BISHOP.
" Norma," " Linda,"

MACREADY.
February 5th and 12th—Concerts for Poor of Dublin at Rotunda*—

                    { Miss SEARLE.
" Israel in Egypt," { Mr. JAMES HILL.
                    { G. L. GEARY, BLANCHARD
                    { Messrs. W. and J. ROBINSON.
Conductor, Mr. R. P. STEWART.†

February 16th—Philharmonic—Mad. DULCKEN, F. ROBINSON, STANFORD.
March 13th—Mrs. BUTLER (F. Kemble).
April 8th—JULIEN and *Pischek* at Music Hall, Abbey Street.
April—CHARLES MATHEWS, Madame VESTRIS, " Farewell engagement."
June 4th—Philharmonic—*Joachim*, " a lad of 14."
———— Miss DOLBY sang " Oh, rest in the Lord !"
Dr. JOHN SMITH appointed Professor of Music, T.C.D.
November 13th—Anacreontic.
December—Mr. and Mrs. CHARLES KEAN.
December 9th—Antients " *Elijah* " (produced at Birmingham, August 26th, 1846)—Miss SEARLE, Mrs. SMITH, STANFORD, R. SMITH, GEARY, F. ROBINSON. Conductor, Mr. J. ROBINSON.

1848 February—Theatre Royal " The Bedouin Arabs !"
(June 15th—CATALANI died at Paris.)

---

* This is remarkable for having combined the performing members of the following Dublin Societies :—Catch Club, Anacreontic, Philharmonic, University Choral, Orpheus, Amateur Harmonic, Amateur Melophonic, Madrigal, Antients, Ladies' Choral, and Philharmonic Brass Band. When will eleven Dublin Musical Societies meet together again in harmony ?
† Afterwards Sir ROBERT STEWART.

A.D.

1848   March 6th—University Choral Society—" *Walpurgis Night.*"

July 81st—" Poses Plastiques," Theatre Royal—Madame
WARTON.

October 10th—Italian Opera (Six nights)—

" Sonnambula," 〔 *Jenny Lind, Roger,*
" Figlia," 〕 F. LABLACHE,
                    Belletti, BOTTARA,
                    BALFE, Conductor.

(Boxes, £1 10s. ; Pit, 12s. 6d.)

——— *Irish Academy of Music* founded.

1849   January 14th—Miss CUSHMAN (after two years), " Fazio."

February 12th—English Opera—

" Bohemian," 〔 Miss RAINSFORTH,
" Bondman," 〕 H. CORRI, W. HARRISON,
" Crown Diamonds, 〕 BORRANI.

February 19th—G. GEARY's Concert—JOSEPH ROBINSON, Miss
Fanny Arthur; played Caprice, SCHULHOFF.

February 28th—Philharmonic—THALBERG.

April—Mr. and Mrs. CHARLES KEAN.

August 8th—Concert for the Queen at Viceregal Lodge—Mr.
and Mrs. H. MACDONNELL, J. STANFORD, Mr. and Mrs. JOSEPH
ROBINSON.

October 12th—Les Sœurs *St. Louin.*

September 13th—Italian Opera—

" Cenerentola," 〔 *Alboni,* CORBARI,
" Figlia," 〕 *Tagliafico,*
" Don Pasquale," 〕 *Polonini.*

October 20th—English Opera—

" Lucia," 〔 *Miss Lucombe,* Miss LANZA,
" Puritani," 〕 DELAVANTI, SIMS REEVES,
" Ernani." 〕 WBITWORTB, HORNCASTLE.

November 6th—Italian Opera—

                    〔 *Catherine Hayes,* Miss POOLE,
" Lucia," 〕 Herr DAMCKE,
" Norma," 〕 Signor BURDINI,
                    〕 *PAGLIERI.

---

* PAGLIERI was hissed off in the first duet. SIMS REEVES, who was in a
private box, was uproariously called for, and came down to the o.p. side of the
stage ; CALCRAFT stood at the other. Then ensued an altercation in which the
audience acted as a (noisy) chorus. At length being told " to shake hands and
make up," he said he would sing to please the audience, " but not Mr. CALCRAFT!"
He dressed, and the Opera went on triumphantly.

A.D.

1850   February 9th—" Richelieu," MACREADY's farewell.

February 11th—Ballet—CARLOTTA GRISI.

February 21st—Italian Opera—

" Sonnambula,"   { C. HAYES, Miss POOLE,
" Linda,"   Miss TRAVERS,
                POLONINI,
                Herr Menghis.

April 22nd—French Opera (Three nights)—

" Domino,"
" Diamants,"   } Madame *Charton* ; MITCHELL.
" Dame Blanche,"

May—Lecture, Theatre Royal—ALFRED BUNN.

June—Ernestine St. Louin, Danseuse at Theatre Royal.

June 11th—English Opera (Ten nights)—

" Bohemian," " Maritana,"   } *Miss Pyne,*
" Crown Diamonds,"   Mr. and Mrs. WEISS,
" Sonnambula,   W. HARRISON, H. CORRI.

October 21st—Italian Opera—

" Sonnambula,"   } C. HAYES, Madame *Macfarren,*
" Linda,"   *Paltoni,* BORDAS,
" Lucrezia,"   MENGHIS,
" Lucia,"   LAVENU, Conductor.

1851   January 5th—Jullien Concerts—*Bottesini, Sivori.*

January 8th—*C. W. Granby* in " She stoops to Conquer."

———— Italian Opera—GRISI announced, but not able to come.

———— English Opera—

" Rob Roy,"   } SIMS REEVES, RICCIARDI,
" Waterman,"   Madame BASSENO,
" Beggar's Opera," } MENGHIS.

July 12th and August 9—* *Mystics.*—First dinners at the Bailey Tavern, on Howth.

December 26th—Mr. JOHN HARRIS opened Theatre Royal as its lessee—" Love in a Maze."

———— Pantomime, " Bluff King Hal."

---

* The following were " *Mystics*":—W. WILDE (" Willie Wildrake"); H. MACDONNELL (" Heinrich"); JOHN CONNELLAN DEANE (" Jack Bishop"); R. THORNTON, R. Artillery; R. P. STEWART, (" Bach"); FK. THORPE PORTER (" Rhadamanthus"); JOHN JONES (" Pygmalion"); JUDGE HALIBURTON, or SAM SLICK; CHARLES GREY; J. F. WALLER (" Jonathan Freke-Slingsby);" THOMAS (ALFRED JONES ; ALEXANDER THOM; JOHN KING (*Saunders*); Dr. MAUNSELL (*Mail*); M'GLASHAN (*University Magazine*), &c., &c.

A.D.

1852 "Amateur Musical Society " founded, with GEORGE J. LEE* as Conductor; JONATHAN ADAIR PHILLIPS, Hon. Secretary.

March 4th—Philharmonic—BOTTESINI, Contrabasso ; SIVORI, Violin.

April 12th—Miss *Charlotte Saunders*, "Prince of Happyland."

May 25th—" *Corsican Brothers*," T. C. KING.

June 10th—Cork Exhibition—Cantata by R. P. STEWART and J. F. WALLER.

September 11th to October 10th—Italian Opera—

" Lucrezia,"	GRISI, MARIO,
" Norma,"	F. LABLACHE, +
" Don Pasquale,"	Susini,
" Puritani,"	GALVANI,
" Don Giovanni,"	MORI, Conductor.

November 8th—*Julia* and *Fanny Cruise* in " Midsummer Night's Dream."

1853 January—JULLIEN at Rotunda—*Anna Zerr*, " Queen of Night;" Herr KŒNIG, Cornet.

At Theatre Royal the Stock Company played 516 nights, without break, alternately Musical and Dramatic pieces (see July 15th, 1854), amongst them :—

" Acis and Galatea,"	Miss LANZA, 2 Misses CRUISE,
" Freyschutz,"	HAIGH, T., DURAND,
" Artaxerxes,"	Miss SEAMAN, ELLEN MORTYN,
" Masaniello,"	Mrs. PARKER, F. Robson,
" Cinderella."	T. C. KING, C. GRANBY, &c.

February 26th— Philharmonic—DORIA and PAUER.

May 12th—Opening of Dargan Exhibition—Choral perform- ance ; † JOSEPH ROBINSON, Conductor.‡

July 5—The Choral Institute—

" Elijah,"	JULIA CRUISE,
	Miss CLARKE,
	G. GEARY, R. SMITH,
	GLOVER, Conductor.

* Afterwards known as G. VANDELEUR LEE.

† The following selection was given :—" Hymn of Praise," and the March from " Athalie," MENDELSSOHN ; " Coronation Anthem," and " Hallelujah," HANDEL; " The Heavens are Telling," and Motett in C., HAYDN; " Hallelujah" from " Mount of Olives," BEETHOVEN; " Hundreth Psalm," and " God Save the Queen," specially arranged.

‡ CHARLES SANTLEY, from Liverpool, was in the Chorus.

A.D.

1853   August 1st—*Alfred Wigan*.

August 31st—Concert for the Queen at Viceregal Lodge—Mr. and Mrs. H. MacDonnell, Miss O'Connor, and Messrs. W., F., and J. Robinson.

October 31st—Closing of Dargan Exhibition.

Jonathan Blewett died, aged 73.

1854   January 6th and 9th—F. W. Brady's Opera Recitals—

"Don Pasquale,"	Mr. and Mrs. H. Macdonnell, Miss Walker, *Ellen Conran*,[*] Dr. F. Robinson, John Stanford.
"Don Giovanni,"	

January 20th—*Arthur Napoleon*, P.F.

February 10, and March 8—"*Paradise and the Peri*," by Schumann.—Julia Cruise, Fanny Cruise, G. Geary, R. Smith, and Ferdinand Glover ; Glover, Conductor.

February 16th—Antients—" St. Paul,"

April 17th—"*Sea of Ice*," E. Mortyn, Corri, Ellerton.

June 14th—Philharmonic—Mad. Julienne, Amadei, *Oberthür*.

July 15th—Presentation to J. Harris, by Company, after playing 516 nights, without interval.

September 11th—Italian Opera—

" Norma,"	*Sophie Cruvelli, Marai,*
" Otello," 13th	Alboni, Signor *Tamberlik,*
"*Fidelio*," 14th	Tagliafico, Polonini,
" Barbiere,"	Santi, Luchesi.
"*Ernani*," 16th	*Alfred Mellon*, Conductor

September 25th—Ellen Conran left for Italy.

October—" Bohemian Girl " played repeatedly.

1855   January 19th—University Choral—"Don Giovanni," H. MacDonnell, &c.

February 27th—Jullien—Madame *Pleyel* and Miss Dolby.

April 9—Helen Faucitt—" Much ado," " Winter's Tale," " As you like it."

May 3rd—Oratorio—" *Abraham*," by Torrance.

May 15 to 19—Italian Opera—

Alboni, Jenny Bauer, Reichardt, Susini.

* Afterwards known as Madame Corani.

1855 August 6th—Italian Opera—

<table>
<tr><td>"Norma,"<br>" D. Pasquale,"<br>" Sonnambula,"<br>" Semiramide,"<br>" Lucrezia,"</td><td>GRISI,
Madame Gassier,
Didiée,
MARIO,
LORINI,
Gassier,
SUSINI,
LI CALSI, Conductor.</td></tr>
</table>

September 7th—Italian Opera—

<table>
<tr><td>" Otello,"<br>" Trovatore," 10th,
" Prophete," 11th.</td><td>Pauline Viardot,
MARAI,
TAMBERLIK,
Graziani,
TAGLIAFICO,
A. MELLON, Conductor.</td></tr>
</table>

September 19th—E. CONRAN's *debut* at Florence.

October 29th to November 10th—English Opera—

<table>
<tr><td>" Fra Diavolo,"<br>" Bohemian Girl,"</td><td>S. REEVES,
Mr. and Mrs. WEISS,
JENNY BAUER,
MANVERS,
FARQUHARSON.</td></tr>
</table>

1856 January 7—Irish Academy of Music re-organized—F. W. BRADY and HERCULES MACDONNELL, Honorary Secretaries.

January 18th—Philharmonic—Ninth Symphony, with chorus, The ROBINSONS and Miss WILLIAMS.

February 1st—Antients—" *Desert*," F. DAVID—E. MORTYN recites.

February 23rd and 25th—Irish Academy of Music—Amateur Opera (Antient Rooms), with Lady *Downshire*, tickets 10s.; " Maritana" realized, net, £474 3s. 2d.

March 24th—VANDENHOFF.

April 4th—Antients—

<table>
<tr><td>" Elijah."</td><td>Mrs. HARPUR,
Mrs. CANTWELL,
Mrs. LEVEY,
R. SMITH,
JOSEPH ROBINSON, Conductor.</td></tr>
</table>

April 9th—Mrs. *Joseph Robinson's* P. F. Recital—Antient Rooms.

A.D.

1856   April 11th—University Choral—" *Eli*," by COSTA—

> Mrs. HARPUR,
> AMADEI,
> GEARY,
> WILLIAM and JOSEPH ROBINSON.

May 12th—" Cymbeline "—HELEN FAUCIT.

May 13th—Catch Club—Experiment tried of admitting ladies behind a screen ! Experiment failed.

May 30th and 31st—Philharmonic—Madame *Clara Wieck Schumann*.

June 18th—Jullien Concerts—Rotunda Gardens.

June 23rd—Antients—Miss DOLBY.

September 15th to 27th—Italian Opera—(BEALE).

> " Ernani,"
> " D. Pasquale,"
> " Lucrezia,"
> " Favorita,"
> " Barbiere,"
> " Trovatore,"
> " Norma."

> GRISI, LORINI, AMADEI,
> Madame GASSIER, MARIO, MEI,
> W. TENNANT, LORINI, ROVERE,
> GRAZIANI, GASSIER, *Formes*,
> LI CALSI, Conductor.

October 14th—Italian Opera—

> " *Traviata*,"
> " Figlia,"
> "Don Pasquale.''

> *Maria Piccolomini*, BERTI,
> *Charles Braham*, ROSSI,
> BELLETTI (BRIZZI).

October 21st—Orchestral Concerts—Antient Rooms—ALFRED MELLON ; Miss JULIA BLEADON, *Picco*. No audience !

October 27th—English Opera—

> LUCY ESCOTT, FANNY HUDDART-DYER,
> AUGUSTUS BRAHAM, H. HAIGH,
> MANVERS, CHARLES DURAND,
> TULLY, Conductor.

November 22nd—Concerts, Rotunda—

> S. REEVES, WEISS, IRVING,
> Mrs. ENDERSOHN.

———— Mr. and Mrs. BARNEY WILLIAMS at Theatre Royal.

November 28th—Philharmonic—HALLÉ, SAINTON, *Piatti*.

December 8th—Five Concerts—Antient Rooms—C. HAYES, Madame CORELLI, CHARLES BRAHAM, WEISS, *Ernst*, PIATTI, GEORGE OSBORNE.

This year, Madame VESTRIS and JOHN BRAHAM died.

A.D.

1857   January 9th—Irish Musical Fund Society—

      "Messiah"   { C. HAYES, and party,
                         { J. ROBINSON, Conductor.

January 13th to 17th—Concerts—C. HAYES.

January 19th to 24th—Jullien.

February 3rd—Antients—Beethoven's "Mass in C" and "The Creation."

March 13th—Mrs. E. GEALE's Puppets—"Trovatore."

March 16th—Italian Operas—

    "Lucia,"
    "Norma,"   } C. HAYES, Mademoiselle CORELLI,
    "Linda,"   } C. *Volpini*, W. TENNANT, *Badiali*,
    "Lucrezia," } *Anschütz*, Conductor.
    "Trovatore."

(April 7th—Opera Company in "Creation" and "Stabat.")

June 15th to 23rd—*W. H. Russell's* Lectures on Crimea, at Theatre Royal.

June 17th—Last dinner of "Mystics," Antient Rooms, to W. H. RUSSELL.

June 23rd—Histrionic Society. Antient Rooms.

August 3rd—Italian Opera—

    "Trovatore,"
    "Lucia,"   Madame *Bosio*, DIDIEÉ,
    "Traviata,"   Madame TAGLIAFICO,
    "Barbiere,"   Victoire *Balfe*,
    "Favorita,"   Signor *Gardoni*, *Neri Beraldi*,
    "Elisire,"   *Ronconi*, GRAZIANI, Zelger,
    "Sonnambula,"   POLONINI, TAGLIAFICO,
    "Puritani,"   ALFRED MELLON, Conductor.
    "*Rigoletto*," August 4th.

August 29th—"Macbetto"—*Ristori*.*

September 21st—Italian Opera—(BEALE)—

    "Trovatore,"
    "*Huguenots*," Oct. 1st.   GRISI,† Madame GASSIER,
    "Traviata,   ALBONI, MARIO, BENEDETTI,
    "Semiramide."   TENNANT, DERIVIZ, BAILLON.

October—Mr. JOHN KNIGHT BOSWELL applied for a theatrical patent, and was refused by Attorney-General J. D. FITZGERALD.

---

* La Marchesa del Grillo.

† Grisi's mother died soon after at Milan.

A.D.

1857   October 10th to 24th—Italian Opera, (LUMLEY and BRIZZI).

      { M. PICCOLOMINI, ORTOLANI, SPEZZIA,* Signor *Giuglini*,† LUCHESI, Belletti, Aldighieri ARDITI, Conductor.

     October 29th—Mr. and Mrs. BARNEY WILLIAMS.

1858   January 11th—JULLIEN, with GRISI!

     January 14th—Philharmonic, with above—WEBER's " *Invitation*," scored by H. BERLIOZ.

     February 1st—Harp Recital, Oberthür—Miss FLYNN, P. F.

     April 19th—University Choral—" A Winter Night's Wake, by R. P. STEWART and J. F. WALLER.

     March—(Theatre Royal re-decorated.)

     April 23rd and 26th—I. A. M. Opera—(Antient Rooms); tickets 10s.

    " Don Giovanni." { Mrs. BENNETT, Miss A. WALKER. Mrs. H. MACDONNELL, Mr. F. ROBINSON, Mr. H. MACDONNELL, J. STANFORD, Major HUME, A. CLOSE, JOSEPH ROBINSON, Conductor.

     May 10th—Antients—

       { JOACHIM, ELSNER, Mrs. JOSEPH ROBINSON, Madame LEMMENS SHERRINGTON.

     May 21st—Philharmonic—*Rubenstein* and Mrs. J. ROBINSON.

     August 11th to 28—Italian Opera—

    " Trovatore," " Lucia," " Traviata," " Figlia," " Sonnambula," " Barbiere," " *La Zingara*," August 16th. | PICCOLOMINI, P. VIARDOT, GIUGLINI, ALDIGHIERI, ARDITI, Conductor.

     November 18th—Miss FLYNN's P. F. Recital.

     December 10th—Philharmonic—PAUER and Mrs. JOSEPH ROBINSON.

     December 18th—CHARLES MATTHEWS—" Used up," "Patter," Clatter," " Cool as a Cucumber."

---

* Married ALDIGHIERI.

† Died 1865, aged 39.

A.D.

1859 January 7th—JULLIEN at Rotunda—*Wieniawski*, Madame A. BISHOP.

January 8th—University Choral Society—

"Walpurgis Night," {Sedlatzek, AMADEI, EDWIN REEVES, ALLAN IRVING.

JANUARY 20th—Philharmonic—JULLIEN, and *Gerhard Taylor*, Harp.

January 31st—Antients—

"Elijah" { JULIA CRUISE, Mrs. LOCKEY, O'RORKE, R. SMITH.

February 21st to 26th—Concerts—(W. BEALE).

{ ARABELLA GODDARD. P. VIARDOT, Miss EYLES, LUCHESI, DRAGONE, REGONDI (Concertina) HATTON, Conductor.

March 28th to April 16th—Italian Opera—

"Norma," { GRISI, P. VIARDOT, SEDLATZEK "Macbetto, April 5th, MARIO, *Corsi*, GRAZIANI, "Marta, April 9th. ARDITI, Conductor.

April 1st—" *Classical Quartett Union* "—Two LEVEYS, WILKINSON, ELSNER.

May 15th (16 nights)—English Opera—PYNE and HARRISON—

" *Rose of Castille*," LANCIA, SEGUIN, " Crown Diamonds, GEORGE HONEY, " *Satanella*," 21st. A. MELLON, Conductor.

May 22nd—Philharmonic—*Leopold de Meyer*, Belart.

May 27th—Antients—HALLE, JOACHIM.

August 6th to 20th—Italian Operas—

"Huguenots," } " Norma," *Therese Tietjens*,* VANERI, " Favorita," GUARDUCCI, GIUGLINI, CORSI, " Trovatore," CASTELLI, BADIALI, *Vialetti*, " Lucia," BOSSI, MERCURIALI, " Barbiere," ARDITI, Conductor. " D. Giovanni." }

September 26th and 28th—Concerts—JENNY LIND, JOACHIM, BELLETTI ; OTTO GOLDSCHMIDT, Conductor.

* Of Hungarian origin, but born at Hamburgh, October 15, 1828. London, 1858; her last performance was at Her Majesty's, in " Lucrezia," May 19, 1877. Died October 3, 1877.

A.D.

1859 October 1st—Italian Opera—(5 nights)—

$$\left\{\begin{array}{l}\text{Piccolomini, Vaneri, Belart,}\\ \text{Corsi, Aldighieri.}\end{array}\right.$$

October 10th—Italian Opera—All, both Tietjens and Picco-lomini, in " D. Giovanni."

$$\left\{\begin{array}{l}\text{Tietjens, Borchardt, Badiali,}\\ \text{Vialetti, Giuglini, Mercuriali.}\end{array}\right.$$

October 27th—Handel Centenary; seats £1 1s.

" Messiah." $\left\{\begin{array}{l}\text{Jenny Lind, Belletti, Mr. \& Mrs.}\\ \text{Lockey, Smith,}\\ \text{J. Robinson, Conductor.}\end{array}\right.$

November 25th—Antients—Madame Rudersdorff, Miss Palmer, George Perren, Thomas, Randegger.

November 28th—Mr. and Mrs. Charles Kean.

December 16th—Philharmonic—Sainton, Piatti, Halle.

1860 January 9th—Antients—" Sons of Art," Mendelssohn.

January 17th—Philharmonic and Beale's Concerts at Rotunda—

$$\left\{\begin{array}{l}\textit{Fiorentini}, \text{Corbari, Badia,}\\ \text{Herr Reichardt, Tagliafico,}\\ \text{Sivori, Bottesini, Herr Engel,}\\ \text{Brinley Richards,}\\ \text{J. L. Hatton, Conductor.}\end{array}\right.$$

March 8th—Italian Opera—

" Nozze." $\left\{\begin{array}{l}\text{Piccolomini, Rudersdorff,}\\ \text{Borchardt, Signor Belart,}\\ \textit{Patey}, \text{Aldighieri, Mercuriali,}\\ \text{Arditi, Conductor.}\end{array}\right.$

March 24th—Retirement of Piccolomini.*

April 23rd—English Opera—Pyne and Harrison—

" Dinorah," May 9th; $\left\{\begin{array}{l}\text{Miss Pilling, Miss Cruise,}\\ \text{Corri, }\textit{Grattan Kelly},\\ \text{A. Mellon, Conductor.}\end{array}\right.$
" Lurline," April 30th.

May 13th—Antients—

" Mass in C." Beethoven $\left\{\begin{array}{l}\text{Madame Sherrington,}\\ \text{Mrs. Cantwell,}\\ \text{Dr. F. Robinson, R. Smith.}\end{array}\right.$

May 31st—Philharmonic—Herr *Lubeck*, P. F.

---

* Soon afterwards became La Marchesa Gaetani della Fargna.

A.D.

1860 June 1st—I. A. M. Amateur Opera Recital—8s.; Rehearsal tickets, 2s. 6d.

"Puritani." { Lady DE VERE, Mrs. EDWARD GEALE, HERCULES MACDONNELL, JOHN STANFORD.

September 10th to 29th—Italian Opera—(W. BEALE)—

"Orfeo." { GRISI, GASSIER, VIARDOT, Mademoiselle ORVILLE, MARIO, GRAZIANI, CIAMPI. VIANESI, Conductor.

November 7th—Philharmonic—CLARA NOVELLO,* MOLIQUE.

November 8th—Antients—

Selections "Messiah" and "Creation" { CLARA NOVELLO, Miss EYLES, CUMMING, LAWLER.

1861 January 15th—F. W. BRADY's "Guy Mannering."

February 21st., and March 2nd—I. A. M. Opera Recital—

"Lucia," "Sonnambula." { Mrs. Magennis, Mr. and Mrs. H. MACDONNELL. JOSEPH ROBINSON, Conductor.

April 1st—(Twenty-four nights)—" Colleen Bawn, Mr. and Mrs. Boucicault.

April 29th—English Opera—PYNE and HARRISON.

September 16th—Italian Opera—

"Il Ballo," 25th. { TIETJENS, LEMAIRE, BELLINI, ANNA WHITTY, GIUGLINI, Della Sedie, BOSSI, CIAMPI.

October 29th—(Six nights)—Italian Opera (Boxes 10s.†)—

"Sonnambula," "Barbiere," "Traviata," "D. Giovanni," "Lucia," "Marta." } Adelina Patti,‡ SEDLATZEK, GALVANI, MANFREDI.

* Married to the Count Giliucci.

† Previous to this, except on extraordinary occasions, a Box seat was but 8s.

‡ Her correct name was Adéla Jeanne Marie. Her mother, Madame Barrili, was a Roman artiste; her father, Salvatore Patti, was a tenor, from Catania; she was born at Madrid, February 19, 1843; her first master was Elisa Valentini, and afterwards Mugio, under whom she made her debut at New York, November 26, 1859; London in 1860; married the Marquis de Caux; 1877 divorced.

1861 November 12th—Death of Dr. John Smith, Professor of Music, T.C.D.

December 3rd—Italian Opera—

"Lucrezia,"
"Rigoletto,"
"Trovatore."
"Sonnambula,"
"Norma,"

} Grisi (*not* Mario), Lemaire, E. Corani, Madame Dario, Galvani, Cresci, Ciampi, Vianesi, Conductor.

December 31st—" Grisi's Farewell"—Norma—Bids adieu to Dublin; but see March, *1866! ! !*

1862 February 7th—Philharmonic and 3 Concerts—*Carlotta* and *Barbara Marchisio*, Arthur Napoleon, Land, Ciampi, *Vieuxtemps.*

February 17th—Mr. and Mrs. Alfred Wigan.

April 9th and 14th—I. A. M. Amateur Opera Recital—

"Marta,"
"Ernani."

{ Mrs. Magenis, Mrs. Wray Palliser, Mr. J. Scott, V. Bartolucci, T. A. Jones, H. MacDonnell, Sir J. Coghill.

April 21st—English Opera—Pyne and Harrison—"Lily of Killarney."

June 24th—Antients—Joachim and Mrs. Joseph Robinson.

Sir R. P. Stewart appointed Professor of Music, T.C.D.

October 2nd to 18th—Italian Opera—

"Trovatore,"
"Lucia,"
"Puritani,"
"D. Giovanni,"
"Sonnambula,"
"Marta,"
"Lucrezia,"
"Norma,"
"Roberto."

} Tietjens, Giuglini, Bossi, Badiali, Formes, Palmieri, Arditi, Conductor.

October———Four Concerts, Rotunda—Miss Sherrington.

November ———Philharmonic—

{ Madame Gassier, A. Goddard, Sainton, Bottesini.

November 17th and 24th—P. F. Recitals—Thalberg.

——————— Theatre Royal—Mr. and Mrs. Charles Kean.

1862 December 15th and 23rd—I. A. M.—Marionettes—
"Bridal of Triermain."
Words—Sir *J. Coghill,* } Julia Cruise, T. A. Jones,
Music—*Alan Close,* } Hugh Kennedy, C. Dollard,
Prologue—H. Macdonnell. } McCreagh.

1863 April 6th—English Opera—Pyne and Harrison.
September 26th—Italian Opera—
"*Faust*," Oct. 1st. { Tietjens, *Trebelli Bettini,* Volpini, Sims Reeves, *Santley,* Bossi.
November 9th—"*Lord Dundreary*—Sothern.
——————— Antients—G. W. Torrance, became Conductor.

1864 February 22nd—"*Ticket of Leave Man.*"
March 8—Granby's Benefit—Captain Lytton as "Hawkesley."
March 28th—"Colleen Bawn," for four weeks.   •
May 2nd—English Opera—Pyne and Harrison—"*She Stoops to Conquer*"—Macfarren.
September 24th—Italian Opera—
} Tietjens, *Clara Sinico,**
} Gardoni, Swift, Santley, Bossi.
October ————— "*David Garrick*"—Sothern.
October 24th—"*Leah*"—Miss Bateman.
November 7th—"*Arrah-na-Pogue*"—Mr. and Mrs. Boucicault.

November 7th—The *Strollers* met, informally, at Captain Henry's. Present—Captain Henry, Sir Joscelyn Coghill, Hercules MacDonnell, Alan Close, Captain Thomson, Hon. T. Bellew, Viscount Southwell.

November—Memorial Window to Sir John Stevenson placed in St. Patrick's by Sir R. P. Stewart.

1865 March 6th to 25th—Italian Opera—●
"Ernani,"
"Faust,"
"Lucrezia," } Tietjens, Veralli, C.,
"D. Giovanni," } Joulain, T. Swift, Santley,
"Norma," } Bossi.
"Fidelio."

* Mademoiselle Clarice Marini; took the name Sinico from her master; in 1874 married Campobello.

A.D.

1865   March 28th—" *Strollers* " regularly founded—
Captain HENRY, LOWRY BALFOUR, Captain THOMPSON, Dr.
NEDLEY, ALAN CLOSE, Sir JOSCELYN COGHILL, C. DOLLARD,
Captain LITTON, Major FORDE, Col. STEWART, Major
MCCREAGH, B. O. COLE, Honorary Secretary.

April 10th—First Strollers' dinner.

April 25th—Antient Rooms, for I. A. M.—

"Bengal Tiger,"   Lady CHARLEMONT,
"Plot and Passion."   Captain LITTON.

May 9th—*Exhibition Palace* opened—Choral Performances—
J. ROBINSON, Conductor.*

June 15th—*Agnes Markham* as Charlotte, in " Stranger."

August 28th—*Buckstone's* Company.

September 13th to October 6th—Italian Opera—
     TIETJENS, SINICO, MARIO,
     SANTLEY, BOSSI.

November 20th—*Toole*—(First time at Theatre Royal—had
played at " Queen's.")

GIUGLINI died, aged 39.

WM. VINCENT WALLACE died, aged 51.

1866   February 2nd—" *London Glee and Madrigal Union* "—
WEBB, BAXTER, COATES, LAND, WINN.

March 3rd—" Strollers "—

"Corsican Brothers,"   P. DU CANE,
     Hon. R. BUTLER,
     Capt. FORTESCUE,
     FINUCANE.

"The Happy Man."   Viscount SOUTHWELL,
     Capt. LITTON,
     Capt. MAHON.

March 12th to 24th—Italian Opera—

"Faust,"   GRISI,† SINICO, Madame DE MERIC
"Norma,"   LABLACHE,
"Lucrezia,"   MARIO, *Caravoglia*, STAGNO, BOSSI,
"Trovatore,"   *Foli*,
"Marta,"   ARDITI, Conductor.
"D. Giovanni."

---

* The Programme included the Old Hundredth Psalm, the Coronation
Anthem, Hymn of Praise, The Heavens are Telling, and The Hallelujah, with
Distin's Great Drum.

† This was GRISI's real retirement from *the stage*. Born at Milan, May 22nd,
1812; *debut* at Vienna with SONTAG, 1828; Milan, January 1st, 1832—Adalgisa
in Norma with PASTA, Paris, 1833; London, April 8th, 1834—Gazza Ladra.

A.D.

1866 March—— *Glee and Madrigal Union* founded—
Miss FENNELL, K. CRUISE, HEMSLEY, TOPHAM, E. PEELE, GRATTAN KELLY.

April 23rd—Philharmonic—*Parepa*, PAUER.

April 26th—Hon. Mrs. *Yelverton's* Readings!—(Miss LONGWORTH.)

May 7th—Re-opening of Exhibition.

"May Cantata"—MACFARREN.} Miss SHERRINGTON,
R. M. LEVEY, Conductor. } FENNELL, TOPHAM, G. KELLY.

May 21st—Cantata "Myra"—Dr. DUNNE—Misses BANKS, and PALMER.

September 11th—Italian Opera—
{ TIETJENS, SINICO, *Baumeister*,
DE MERIC LABLACHE, *Zandrina*,
MARIO, MORINI, GASSIER, BOSSI,
FOLI, SANTLEY, TOM. HOHLER,
ARDITI, Conductor.

October 29th—Madame *Beatrice* in "Mary Stuart."

1867 January 7th—Lady NAAS' Amateur Concert — (JOSEPH ROBINSON, Conductor).

———— Glee and Madrigal Union modified—
{ Miss FENNELL, PEELE, HEMSLEY,
R. SMITH, and G. KELLY.

September —— Italian Opera—
{ TIETJENS, SINICO, DORIA,
BAUMEISTER, DE M. LABLACHE,
T. HOHLER, TOMBESI, GASSIER,
FOLI, SANTLEY.

October —— T. C. KING re-appeared, after 12 years.

December 31st—Strollers dined at Antient Rooms—First Printed Programme.

1868 March 25th and 26th*—"Monthly Popular Concerts"—
Chamber Classical Music, { JOACHIM, LEVEY, HATTON,
ELSNER.

* These continued till 1871. The following artists appeared:—HALLE, PAUER, KUHE, JOACHIM.

A.D.

1868   March 28th—HARRIS's Benefit—"Still Waters," "Bombastes, '
C. DOLLARD.

March 31st—Amateur Opera—

"Trovatore." { Miss *Annie Doyle*, L. E. SHAW,
M. LEVEY, Messrs. J. MARLOWE,
P. *Hayes, Charles Cummins*,
MONTGOMERY,
G. J. LEE, Conductor.

April 18th—Installation of PRINCE of WALES at St. Patrick's—
Dr. FRANCIS ROBINSON, Conductor.

May 9th—"Strollers."

"Guy Mannering,"

"Teddy the Tiler." { Miss GIFFORD,
Miss HINTON,
W. BENTHAM,
C. DOLLARD,
P. HAYES,
Capt. MAHON,
LETABLERE LITTON.

September 14th to October 31st—Italian Opera—

"Trovatore,"
"Huguenots,"
"Fidelio."
"Faust,"
"Norma,"
"Oberon."
"Nozze," } TIETJENS, TREBELLI, BAUMEISTER,
ZANDRINA, SINICO, *Mongini*,
SANTLEY, FOLI, TAGLIAFICO,
FORMES; ARDITI and BEVIGNANI,
Conductors.

1869   January 13th—Readings at Rotunda—*Charles Dickens*.
March 8th—

"Stabat Mater "* { Mrs. SHAW,
Miss LYONS,
P. HAYES,
H. MACDONNELL,
G. J. LEE, Conductor.

———————— "Hamlet"—BANDMANN.
April 1st—"Leah"—Miss BATEMAN.

* Rossini's Stabat had been often previously performed in Dublin, but I do
not happen to have the dates. In London it was first produced, on a moderate
scale, by Balfe, April 29, 1842. The basses were Weiss and H MacDonnell.

A.D.

1869   September 13th to October 9th —Italian Opera—

" Huguenots,"
" Faust,"
" Dinorab,"   TIETJENS, *Ilma di Murska,*
" Roberto,"   *Scalchi*, SINICO, BAUMEISTER,
" Zauberfloëte,"   GARDONI, SANTLEY, GASSIER,
" Linda,"   DELLA ROCCA,
" Marta,"   MONGINI, *Bagagiolo,* ZOBOLI,
" Freyschütz,"   ARDITI and VIANESI, Conductors.
" Fidelio,"   ROSALIA, Danseuse.
" Trovatore."

October 7th—" Messe Solennelle."

November 8th—Nilsson Festival—

" Messiah " Selections.   *Christine Nilsson*, Madame DRASDILL,
Nov. 9th, " Creation."   SIMS REEVES, FOLI; HENRY LESLIE,
Nov. 13th, " Stabat."   Conductor.   Sir R. STEWART,
Stalls, £1 1s.   Organist.

December 10th—Philharmonic—*Norman Neruda.*

1870   January 25th to 28th—Philharmonic and Exhibition Concerts—   TIETJENS.

March 14—French Opera
Bouffe—   *Schneider,*
" La Grande Duchesse,"   VIZENTINI, Conductor,
" Barbe Bleu,"   RAPHAEL FELIX, Manager.
" Orphée,"

March 28th—Philharmonic—" Son and Stranger."

April 6th—" Strollers,"—}   Capt. BOWEN, COLLINS, Major
" Follies of a Night," }   HALL.

" Sentinel,"   } T. FAGAN, P. HAYES, C. DOLLARD,
         }   W. BENTHAM.

April 9th—Amateur Opera—G..V. LEE,
    " Faust."—Mrs. SHAW, GABBET, HAYES and MARLOWF,

May—BELLEW's Readings, Rotunda,

May 14th—GRANBY's benefit.
" The Rivals,"   Capt. BOWEN.

" Waterman,"   } " The Strollers,"
         } T. FAGAN, C. DOLLARD, &c.

————— I. A. Music receives Government Grant of £150 a year.

C

A.D.

1870   Sept. 12th to Oct. 1st—Italian Opera —

"Trovatore," "Barbiere," "Masaniello," "Norma," "Sonnambula," "D. Giovanni," "Nozze," "Faust," "Huguenots," "Lucia."	TIETJENS, BAUMEISTER, SINICO, Madame *Leon Duval*, Miss *Madigan*, TREBELLI, SCALCHI, BETTINI, *Vizzani, Rinaldini, Fancelli, Cotogni,* CARAVOGLIA, CIAMPI, TAGLIAFICO. BEVIGNANI, Conductor. *Ricois*, Danseuse.

October 20th, Thursday—Death of M. W. BALFE, at Rowney Abbey, Herts.

1871   Am. Concert for French wounded, February 27th, "The Strollers" assist.

    March 11th—Am. Opera—

"Marta."	Miss DOYLE, Mrs. DOYLE, P. HAYES, CHARLES CUMMINS. GEORGE V. LEE, Conductor.

    September—T. R.—"School," and "Caste"—

    September 11th to 30th—Italian Opera—

"Trovatore," "Anna Bolena," "Sonnambula," "Semiramide," "Barbiere," "Figlia," "Flauto," "Roberto," "Oberon."	TIETJENS, BAUMEISTER, COLOMBO, *Marie Marimon, Fernandez* (Mrs. BENTHAM), ILMA DI MURSKA, TREBELLI, VIZZANI, RINALDINI, ZOBOLI, *Agnesi, Mendioroz,* FOLI, LI CALSI, Conductor. Ricor Danseuse.

    October 26th—"*Choral Class*" founded at I. A. M.—Jos. ROBINSON, Conductor.

    November 27th—"*Gaiety Theatre*" opened in King Street by MICHAEL and JOHN GUNN—

        "She Stoops to Conquer."

        ————W. B. MARTIN became Conductor of the "Strollers.'

A.D.

1872   February 28th—*Sir Robert* PRESCOTT STEWART knighted.

March 2nd—" Strollers,"—

"Maritana."
{
BLANCHE COLE,
Miss ADA TRAVERS,
CHARLES CUMMINS,
P. HAYES,
W. B. MARTIN,
C. DOLLARD,
CH. MARTIN.
}

May 16th—First *I. A. M. Choral Concert*—Antient Rooms—
I. " God is Love."   Mrs. JOS. ROBINSON,
II. Miscellaneous.   JOS. ROBINSON, and Mr. O'DONOHUE,
Conductors.

May 21st—" Strollers."—

" Retribution."
{
ADA TRAVERS,
Capt. BOWEN,
Major HALL,
GORDON,
P. HAYES.
}

" The Sentinel,"
{
Miss MARKHAM,
Capt. FLEMING,
P. HAYES,
C. DOLLARD.
}

June 5th—Exhibition—" Inauguration Ode,"—WALLER and STEWART.

June 6th—Exhibition—I. A. M. Concert—H. R. H. Duke of Edinburgh.

September 30th to October 19th—Italian Opera—

" Don Pasquale,"
" Don Giovanni,"
" Lucia,"
" Marta,"
" Huguenots,"
" Sonnambula,"
" Semiramide."
{
TIETJENS,
I: DI' MURSKA,
MARIMON,
TREBELLT,
BETTINI,
AGNESI,
Campanini,
MENDIOROZ.
LI CALSI, Conductor.   (RICOIS, Danseuse.)
}

I. A. M. made *"Royal Irish Academy of Music."*

Oct 20th—Death of Dr. FRANCIS ROBINSON.

A.D.

1873　January 6th—" New Philharmonic Society,"—Conductor, G. VANDELEUR LEE—

" Stabat Mater." $\left\{\begin{array}{l}\text{TIETJENS,}\\\text{SINICO,}\\\text{MACVITZ,}\\\text{TOMBESI,}\\\text{AGNESI,}\end{array}\right.$

January 11th—" Messiah,"—Same Company,

March 22nd—" Strollers,"—

" The Brigand," $\left\{\begin{array}{l}\text{Miss WALLIS,}\\\text{Capt BOWEN,}\\\text{P. HAYES,}\\\text{W. BENTHAM,}\\\text{C. MARTIN.}\end{array}\right.$

" Weather permitting,"　Major SNOW.

March 31—Amateur Performance at Mrs. BANKS—

" Paradise and the Peri," by Schumann. $\left\{\begin{array}{l}\textit{Miss Hanlon,}\\\text{B. HERBERT,}\\\text{SHELLEY,}\\\text{JULIA HARRIS,}\\\text{E. PEELE,}\\\text{P. HAYES,}\\\text{B. MULLEN,}\\\text{J. ROBINSON, Conductor.}\end{array}\right.$

At Judge Monahan's, " Mirella." $\left\{\begin{array}{l}\text{BESSIE CRAIG, T. BELLEW, E. PEELE.}\\\text{HEMSLEY, Conductor.}\end{array}\right.$

May 14th—Exhibition—

" Athalie." $\left\{\begin{array}{l}\text{EDITH WYNNE,}\\\text{De MERIC LABLACHE,}\\\text{OTTO ALVSLEBEN,}\\\text{G. V. LEE, Conductor.}\end{array}\right.$

———— Exhibition—Orchestral Concerts, by LEVEY—(Well done, but failed to pay)!

———— Glee and Madrigal modified : Mrs. SCOTT FENNELL, Mr. E. PEELE, and Mr. HEMSLEY, retiring.

August 12th—RISTORI—" Medea,"

August 26th—Gaiety—Italian Opera—

" Lucrezia," " Trovatore," " Norma," " Ballo," " D. Giovanni," " Barbiere," " Faust," " Marta," $\left\{\begin{array}{l}\textit{ELENA CORANI,}\\\textit{Ida Corani,}\\\text{MARIMON,}\\\textit{Miss Sinclair,}\\\text{De M. LABLACHE,}\\\text{BETTINI,}\\\text{CELLI,}\\\text{FOLI,}\\\text{TAGLIAFICO.}\end{array}\right.$

1873 September 15th to October 4th—T. R. Italian Opera—

"Favorita,"	TIETJENS,
"Marta,"	SINICO,
"Trovatore,"	Marie Roze,
"Norma,"	TREBELLI,
"Faust,"	A. Valleria,
"Oberon,"	MAOVITZ,
"Barbiere,"	Urio,
"Flauto,"	ARAMBURO,
"Nozze,"	AGNESI,
"Lucia,"	MENDIOROZ,
	CAMPOBELLO,
	Perkins,
	ZOBOLI,
	BORELLA.

LI CALSI, Conductor,   RICOIS, Danseuse.

1874 February 28th—Levey's Benefit—

"Guy Mannering."
  BESSIE HERBERT,
  BESSIE CRAIG,
  AGNES MARKHAM,
  C. DOLLARD,
  DONNELLY,
  McNEVIN,
  J. P. RYAN.

March 19th—Funeral of JOHN HARRIS, Lessee of T. R.

———— Messrs. MICHAEL and JOHN GUNN take Theatre
Royal.

May 4th—Meeting at Mansion House to place Balfe Memorial
Bust in National Gallery. Sir RICHARD MACDONNELL,
K.C.M.G., C.B., &c., in chair. Not done till July 6th, 1878.

May 13th—" Strollers "—

"Wonder."
  Capt. BOWEN,
  W. BENTHAM,
  C. MARTIN.

" Mr. Bulliondust's
  Legacy," by NUGENT
  ROBINSON.
  H. KENNEDY,
  JOHN McDERMOTT,
  JERRY PERRY,
  C. DOLLARD.

May 15th—Exhibition—R. I. A. M. Choral Concert—
Haydn's Imperial Mass,
42nd Psalm—
2s. 6d. Reserved. 1s. Unreserved. Jos. ROBINSON, Conductor.

A.D.

1874 June 2nd—ELSNER's Concert—" Strollers" assist.

June 11th—BALFE's " Talismano" produced at Drury Lane—
CHRISTINE NILSSON and MARIE ROZE.

July 6th—Opera Bouffe—
" La Fille de Madame } PATTIE LAVERNE,
    Angot." } JULIA MATHEWS.

August 17th—Gaiety—English Opera—
              { ROSE HERSEE,
" Bohemian,"   { PERREN,
" Maritana,"   { CORRI,
              { A. COOKE.
(R. LEVEY, Conductor.)

September to October 10th—Italian Opera—
          { TIETJENS,
          { MARIE ROZE,
          { A. VALLERIA,
          { RISARELLI,
" Huguenots,"   { TREBELLI,
" *Talismano*," Oct. 3rd.   { De M. LABLACHE,
" *Catarina*,"   { *Singelli*,
" *Flauto*,"   { BAUMEISTER,
" Semiramide," &c.,   { CAMPANINI,
" Marta."   { BENTHAM,
          { GIULIO PERKINS,
          { *De Reschi*,
          { *Galassi*,
          { *Behrens*.

October—" *Instrumental Music Club* "* founded—Dr. F. R.
CRUISE, J. F. ELRINGTON, JOHN STANFORD, T. FARRELL, HENRY
E. DOYLE, H. VIVIAN YEO.

November 16th—*Carlotta* PATTI—

1875 February 11th—" Royal Hibernian Academy "—Their first
Exhibition dinner—" Strollers" attend.

February 24th—R. I. A. M. Choral Concert—Exhibition—
" Beethoven's Mass in C." Jos. ROBINSON, Conductor.

———— Additional grant of £100 a year to R. I. A. M.

March 4th—LEVEY's Benefit. } BESSIE HERBERT, McNEVIN,
" Rob Roy." } T. DONNELLY.

* Popularly better known as '' The Scrapers," or " Catgut."

A.D.

1875 March 29th to April 17th—English Opera—

"Bohemian."

> Julia Gaylord,
> Louise Durand,
> A. THIRLWALL,
> Mr. and Mrs. A. COOKE,'
> Packard,
> H. Nordblom,
> CELLI,
> LUDWIG,*
> Carl ROSA, Conductor.

April 9th—Am. Performance at Mrs. Banks. "Faust" by Schumann.

April 30th—Phil.—SINICO, CAMPOB'ELLO, B. McGUCKIN, DUVERNOY, P. F.

June 2nd—"Strollers"—First Ladies' Concert, Antient Rooms

June 21—T. R.—24 Promenade Concerts—KARL MEYDER.

June 25th—R. I. A. M.—Last Choral Concert—(American Rifle Team attend)—

"L'Allegro,"
"Athalie."—Jos. ROBINSON, Conductor.

July—Madge Robertson—"Pygmalion."

July 26th—COULON's French Opera Troupe—

"Les Mousquetaires,"
"La Dame Blanche,"
"Zampa,"
"Guillaume Tell."

August 5th—Exhibition—O'Connell Centenary—

"Elijah".—Jos. ROBINSON, Conductor.

August 7th—"Tara,"—GLOVER.

September 13th—TIETJENS, "Farewell Concerts," going to America.

October 4th to 23rd—Italian Opera—

"D. Giovanni,"
"Figlia,"
"Lohengrin,"
"Dinorah,"
"Trovatore,"
"Sonnambula,"
"Fra Diavolo,"
"Favorita,"
"Puritani."

> Albani,
> Bianchi,
> D'Edelsberg,
> Zare Thalberg, †
> Naudin,
> Maurel,
> MEDICA,
> Pavani,
> VIANESI, Conductor.

* Son of Mr. Ledwyche of T. R.
† Daughter of Elena d'Angri, wife of Senor Pedro de Abella.

A.D.

1875   October 13th—Concerts, Exhibition—CHRISTINE NILSSON—

————— R. I. A. M. Choral Class discontinued, and *Dublin Musical Society* formed in its stead.

November 15th to 20th—Italian Opera—

"Faust,"
" Marta,"

{ CHRISTINE NILSSON (first appearance in Opera here)
ELENA VARESI,
TREBELLI,
Madame LABLACHE,
GILLANDI,
GALASSI,
DEL PUENTE.

November 22nd—SOTHERN—

December 6th to 18th—English Opera—CARL ROSA—

" Trovatore,"
" Maritana,"
" Siege of Rochelle,"
" Fra Diavolo,"
" Bohemian,"
" Zampa,"
" Faust."

{ TORRIANI,
JOSEPHINE YORKE,
F. PACKARD,
LUDWIG,
SANTLEY.

1876   March 13th—Italian Opera—CAMPOBELLO Impressario !—

" Sonnambula,"
" Flauto,"
" Huguenots,"
" Trovatore,"
" Rigoletto,"
" Freischutz,"
" William Tell,"
" D. Giovanni,"
" Maritana," (first time in Italian.)

{ Madame CAMPOBELLO SINICO,
Emma Howson,
Madame *Laville Ferminet,*
DE M. LABLACHE,
VIZZANI,
ROCCA,
Lalloni,
URIO,
FOLI,
ZOBOLI,
LI CALSI, Conductor.

March 16th—GLOVER's " Tara."

March 31st—VERDI's *Requiem.*

April 6th—Dublin Musical Society—Exhibition—

I. " Hymn of Praise,"
II. Miscellaneous.

{ E. WYNNE,
Mrs. SCOTT,
B. MCGUCKIN,
OLDHAM,
Jos. ROBINSON, Conductor.

A.D.

1876 April 30th—LEVEY's Benefit—

"Honeymoon,"
"No Song, no Supper."
{ BESSIE CRAIG,
Mrs. HORSMAN,
A. MARKHAM,
TERESA BELLEW,
McNEVIN,
C. DOLLARD,
DONNELLY,
J. P. RYAN. }

April 21st—"Strollers,"—Ladies' Soirée—Rotunda.
April 17th to 24th—*Salvini*—"Otello,"—
May 6th—GUNN's Benefit—Opera Bouffe—

"*Rhampsinitus*," by
Cellini.
{ Miss T. BELLEW,
E. THOM,
McNEVIN,
CROTTY,
OLDHAM. }

April 29th—Dublin Musical Society—
"St. Cecilia Mass," GOUNOD. Jos. ROBINSON, Conductor.

———— "Glee and Madrigal Union" dissolved.

[WAGNER Festival at Bayreuth—
Rehearsals, June 3rd to August 1st.
Performances, August 3rd to August 30th.*]

September 23rd—Amateur Performance—Gaiety—

"Naval Engagements,"
"No Song no Supper,"
"Cousin Fred," by
Miss Beauchamp.
{ BESSIE CRAIG,
TERESA BELLEW,
McNEVIN,
A. MANNING,
C. DOLLARD, &c. }

September 25th to October 7th—Italian Opera—

"Barbiere,"
"Norma,"
"Semiramide,"
"Lucia,"
"Trovatore,"
"Nozze."
{ TIETJENS,
ALWINA VALLERIA,
TREBELLI,
MARIE ROZE,
BAUMEISTER,
RINALDINI,
Dorini,
GILLANDI,
DEL PUENTE,
ROCCA,
BROCCOLINI,
BEHRENS. LI CALSI, Conductor. }

* The contingent attending from Ireland consisted of Sir R. P. Stewart,
C. Villiers Stanford—De Versan—T. Mayne and Hercules Macdonnell.

D

1876   October 24th — Gaiety—"*Rip Van Winkle*," — JOSEPH
      JEFFERSON.

      October 24th and 27th—Concerts—ALBANI, ZARE THALBERG.
      VIANESI, Conductor.

      November 16th—P. F. Recitals—ARABELLA GODDARD.

      ——————— " The Bells,"—IRVING.

      December 16th—Dublin Musical Society—
        I. " St. Paul,"—
        II. " Resurrection,"—CHAS. V. STANFORD.   JOS. ROBINSON,
        Conductor.

      December 27th—Gaiety—

        " *Shaughraun*."   { MISS *Eveleen Rayne*,
                            { Mr. HUBERT O'GRADY.

INDEX.

www.ingramcontent.com/pod-product-compliance
Lightning Source LLC
Chambersburg PA
CBHW021553270326
41931CB00009B/1195